no crown, no title: a mixtape of tho(ugh)ts

CARLA AARON-LOPEZ

SMG | Books

A division of Shalimar Media Group, LLC

Atlanta, Georgia

www.smgbooks.com

Cover design by Sean Fahie

Carla Aaron-Lopez

Copyright © 2014 Carla Aaron-Lopez

All rights reserved.

ISBN: 0692339523
ISBN-13: 978-0692339527

CONTENTS

no crown, no title: a mixtape of tho(ugh)ts

SIDE A - LIFE

prologue - intro about being stuck in the middle and introduction of writer

1 - ppd sucks - about being stupid, making bad decisions, changing your mind and recognizing that you've got to chase your dreams

2 - what?! where am i? - being back home and learning to take advantage of life

3 - alone in the dark at 2am - ~~defining the breaking point and why rejection is great~~

4 - on being an artist - How do I explain what I do for a living to someone else?

5 - their eyes stopped watching god - when philosophy and pop culture meet southern storytelling (shit that goes through my mind when I attempt new bodies of work)

SIDE B

6 - heres to you, anthony bourdain - aspirations to be just like anthony bourdain

7 - THOTs & ratchetry - the evolution of slang in pop culture, American morality and human sexuality (why *of gods & monsters* is an important body of work by a woman artist)

8 - in defense of niggadom - combine two blog entries: a response to kara walker's a subtlety & the negro as modern day spectacle

9 - space is the place - see blog entry on escapism & afrofuturism and experiencing afropunks in atl

10 - in kurt we trust - the aftermath of grunge - see blog entry

an epilogue of i love yous & fuck yous

prologue
#nowplaying: SZA feat. Kendrick Lamar - Babylon

I've always wanted to do this but never had a clue how to start the motherfucker. I figured just start. That's what other people say in terms of writing a book. This isn't a memoir as if some great part of my life is over. Nor is this a great realization of some life shit. I like to think of this as the middle as I conduct my time in suburgatory (*suburb* + *purgatory*). I'm not introducing myself. Just my voice so you can put my shoes on your feet and walk around for a while. I want you to see what I see. Be able to hear what I hear and all the other senses. If you still have the ability to play with your imagination then I believe that you can. It's one the last few treasures that we have as humans. Therefore, imagine that you are sitting in someone else's blue office chair in a theater classroom in a North Carolina high school on the edges of the city of Charlotte. There are no students. Just lilac walls and empty chairs of a theater classroom. You're dying for the nicotine of a menthol cigarette and more caffeine. You just found out about SZA and can't stop playing *Babylon* on repeat. You get lost in the bassline of the song. Just daydreaming.

Cru-crucify me.
Crucify.
Cru-cru.

Dreaming about places you'd rather be and the kind of person you wish you were. But reality shifts back as a group of kids are playing in the hall and you remember that you're a lonely substitute teacher waiting for children to show up after they're finished with their finals. You think about past adventures. You're envious of tweets about last night's follies with friends you miss in cities across the US. You make love to strangers you've seen walking the streets in slow motion in your mind to the repeating song playing in the background. You wish you could look like *that girl* you saw on Instagram last night. The song ends. Damn. Click. Repeat again.

I can't recall the last time I took advice from anyone.
Shaped like a figure eight who trusts pretty girls anyway?http://rapgenius.com/2898766/Sza-babylon/Who-trusts-pretty-girls-anyway
And I can't recall the last time I took advice from anyone.
I'm sure I'll be the death of me.

God. It's just 908a. I know I'm not the only one in this building that feels like this. My daydreams are worse than my nightmares. They're what I want more than anything. But in reality I have a son that I take care of, debts that need to be paid and the quiet of this lonely classroom. Can't you see it? Are you here yet? Or are you sitting in front of your computer, tablet, smartphone reading these words agreeing with me? Are you sitting in your office or cubicle agreeing with me? If you're like me right now then all we have are our dreams. Do you wish you were walking barefoot on sandy beaches holding your drink of choice? Is it alcoholic or not? Do you have on clothes? I don't know. But I'm talking to you.

Are you hating yourself?
Do you really hate me?
Are you hating yourself?

I chose to start in the middle because that's a place we often end up in or stop altogether. It's like walking the crossroads of Mississippi and instead of picking a direction to go toward you just sat down. There's still a journey ahead of you but you're not sure of where to go. You've come from somewhere but you haven't looked back or given enough thought to what happened back there. These words are my thoughts of what's happened back there, over there and right here. I've sat down but I'm not waiting for Godot. I've sort of placed myself in a self-induced purgatory because I'm not sure what to do next. I'm writing because my dreams have been rather odd. At night I keep dreaming that I'm in these open fields with different variables surrounding me. I can't figure out which way to go but I do know that I can't go back to the past. That would be Hell. Repeating the same actions over and over again because I never learned the first time. Do y'all feel me? Where are you? Where do you want to go? Are we there together? Maybe I'll see you in passing, too. It's my hopes that we share a beer and our own versions of war tales about our lives. I'm sure we'll be entertained.

I'd eventually get drunk and let words flow from my mouth with no control. I'd get emotional and so would you. We're stuck in the middle together and this is a prologue to a book about getting older in America. Fuck.

Cross my heart then I hope to die with a peace of mind (a peace of mind).
Piece together my brain soon as this beat rewind (beat rewind).
Nitrogen and propane I spike your drink at times (turn up, turn up).
I make it hard to swallow this game, you throw up every line.
I notice people got Napoleon complexes, that's my confession.
You said that we're equal but I know you're beyond guessing that I'm beyond desperate (yeah that).
6AM on a Friday morning, my darkest hours,
Them heartless hours.
My apartment is lost in a coffin.

Let me give you a hug. Let me kiss you. Let me be your worshipped king for one night. I'm only human and so are you. We're not gods. Just folk trying to figure this thing out. No matter our race, religion or socioeconomic status. When morning comes, so do I and so do you. We'll return to our normal lives. I'll be a substitute teacher in an empty classroom. You'll return to wherever you came from. We'll be back in the middle. Stuck. Until one of us makes a move in a direction.

Was it worth it?

Would you do it again?
Aren't you tired of always making amends?
I know you hate me now.
I bet you hate me now.
Bring on the thorny crown.
Crucify me.

So I welcome you to the beginning of an idea, a concept of words and songs pulled together about a period of life that I'm not finished walking through. Or maybe, this is my beginning to something. I will not truly know the repercussions of this project until I am finished but when I get there I'll let you know. I've been a writer since 2002 and I know how to command words. I've been an artist my entire life and I believe in the power of communicating yourself visually. They are all I know in this life. And right now the middle is the best place to start.

I'm really over the cryin' thing, wipin' my tears.
Who cries anyway?
Spread like disease all over me
We did ungodly ghastly things, last night I mean.
Who's God anyway?
You're mine any day.
It's burning,
Take me.
I wanna feel
Your power
This final hour.
Tell me,
Are you losing yourself?
Will you lose it for me?
Are you losing yourself?

End prologue song.

Begin mixtape - **no crown, no title: a mixtape of tho(ugh)ts.**

SIDE A:
1. ppd sucks

#nowplaying: Big KRIT - Down & Out, Viktorious

When I woke up I was in a different state. Back in my hometown and about 50 lbs lighter than when I left years previous. It took me a while to get reacquainted with my surroundings again. Actually, I'm not sure what just happened between 2011 and 2013. That part of my life is a big blur and only key memories pop up at random times. I think I'm shell-shocked from having a baby. 2013 was the longest and worst year of my life to date. A lot of it I can really do without.

This sucks and life sucks. Am I going through post-partum depression this bad?

That's all I can remember thinking for months. I damn near destroyed everything that I loved or at least liked/tolerated. I lost my job in December 2012 then my car in March 2013. My mom came during summer 2013 and took my son to North Carolina with her because one day while I was sitting in my former institution, I wrote a suicide note for all of Facebook to see. It was at that point that I didn't care about life anymore. She actually did me a favor with that one. I needed to be alone but when she left I screamed out of anger and frustration for days. I was a walking 30 year old ticking time bomb with nothing but time, weed and whiskey on my hands. I stayed that way for months. When she convinced me to come home in September, I concocted a bullshit plan for my apartment because I left Atlanta knowing I wanted to turn right back around and go back. I allowed one of my boyfriend's hideous friends to move in and convinced a stupid girl to live in this small ass 800 sq. foot space until I returned.

What. The. Fuck. Was. I. Thinking? I still had self-destruction on my mind.

I created my own self-destruct in that moment because my screaming episodes didn't stop for a long while. I set off a bomb in my own home, returned to Atlanta and set off another bomb in my apartment. I cleared that motherfucker out like a woman trying to desperately find peace in a cacophonous world of voices. It served as a representation of everything I had never wanted at that point. The fact that I had said yes to many things I did not want. The fact that I'm always the listener for what I should do with my life instead of just doing what I want. The fact that I lost control over what little I did have in my life. Metaphorically speaking, I burned everything to start over. I needed sacrifices for this experimental spell I was creating. Lambs for the slaughter, my love and my family. I walked away from a relationship I loved being in. But our mediocrity was killing me slowly and I was ignoring that part. My family was very disappointed with the decisions I was making. I wasn't listening to them because I had determined that they felt overbearing. As for the girl I invited in, I should've just fucked her and moved on instead of dragging her along. To this day, what happened to between her and my then boyfriend isn't her fault. I set that up to happen and got mad when they fucked without me being there, too. And who was the stupid girl in the end? Both of us.

I need to start over. Press reset. No repeat.

I made my bed and laid in it. I ate hateful thoughts and words for breakfast, lunch and dinner. I quenched my thirst with cheap beer. I had hit a new level of low and I had no more lies to tell. Especially to myself. *PPD sucks.* They never really tell you about that bit when you get pregnant. The projected image is that you'll be so elated and grateful for this new addition when really you have to learn about taking care of another human as much as they have to learn how to deal with not only your crazy ass but also how to survive in this world. In the mean time, you're on automatic making sure your new baby is alright. You feed, change and clothe him, her or them if you have more than one. You'll take them to the doctor for check-ups and shots because that's what new parents are supposed to do. You lose sleep when they cry in the middle of the night because you're scared to death that if they cry too much while living in an apartment that someone will call Child Protective Services on you. Or at least, that's how my mom would scare the shit out of me through phone calls and visits here and there.

I'm slowly drowning and I don't know what to do.

I believe that's when all of this got started. Not with her phone call but with the descent I was on since 28 July 2012. I gave birth to my first child and what a hell of an experience. I never knew it was like that. I had never been through so many emotional ups and downs. And I never want to return to that place again. I'd even trade in all the sleepless nights to almost never be pregnant again. But if I don't walk through that process I will not be able to have a beautiful child that I helped to create again. And boy, what a beautiful boy I helped to create. Yes. He is the reason why I write these words because I have a big responsibility on my hands. Not only do I have to feed and clothe this little man but I also have to show him how to live a fulfilled life. If I can't show him that then what am I doing in life? It can't always be smoky days and drunken nights while having conversation after conversation with strangers saying I'm something that I'm not even devoting proper time to develop. I'm an artist and a writer. How will I prove this to him? By getting out this emotional/hormonal rut first. Second, clean my act up because no one ever wants a permanent bachelor for a mother. Lastly, prove to myself and him that we can conquer whatever we want in the name of our kingdom, our family.

If I keep being stupid and keep making bad decisions then none of these new dreams will come true. I tried to hold on to my self-proclaimed dirty hipster life in Atlanta depending on my family to do the parts I should've been doing myself. However, when night would turn into day and I was left with hangovers and nothing but time to think, reality would sit in my bedroom like a monster staring at me. *You're finally alone now. What's next? More of this? More no money for food and bills but money for weed and beer days? How long are you going to run from my cousin, Responsibility?* My final straw came on a night when that same hideous dude I was sharing my apartment with decided to sexually assault me in my sleep. I didn't need to stay or think longer in order to move on. That was it. I'm done here.

When you begin to take full responsibility for your life, you have to take responsibility for every little thing, good and bad, that you have done. He should've never been there but I allowed that. All the people that stayed in my apartment that same summer should've never been there but I allowed that. My son should've never left his family but I allowed that. I allowed a lot of ridiculous things to happen and I paid for it. When I found out I was going to lose my apartment, it felt like a proverbial weight had been lifted from my shoulders and helped the letting go process move along. The property manager had enough of my bullshit and I can see why. I bounced before I had a sheriff knocking at my door. Goodbye, Atlanta. The tears are falling down my face as a leave a section of the United States that feels too much like where I belong. But I have bigger issues that need to be conquered before

I return to the beautiful Southern glory that is you. Resurgens. I will come back to you.

21 December 2013. Back in Charlotte. Again.

Here I am. Again. I came back with a bottle of Jamaican rum ready to douse my problems. Christmas came and went. Then New Year's Eve. I cracked her open and drank until early morning. Somewhere in between all that liquor I decided to wake up the next day as a different person. The change had to forcibly come by my hands because I was starting over. No shitty days because I woke up in a decidedly shitty mood. No evilness to my family because I was starting over in the home I left behind. No more blaming myself for the mistakes I had made. Just move on, kid. Most people don't get to have a second chance therefore I need to take mine by the balls. I started making art and writing again. I got my priorities straight and started applying for more jobs again. I was unemployed for 14 months and amazingly after all the struggle I went through in Atlanta I finally became employed again at home. I became a substitute teacher for Charlotte-Mecklenburg Schools and I love it because I'm fucking working again. When you're someone that has worked for half of their life at 30, you tend to go crazy when all of a sudden you don't have a job and you're not in school.

So what's next, you think. I'M GONNA TAKE OVER THE FUCKING WORLD!

No. I'm not… yet. I'm going to face my problems and work on each one as if they're math word problems like I'm in school again. I've learned that successful people always face their problems. And they always seem to do it with a cool head on their shoulders. I wanted to do the same. Therefore, each day is presented with a new set of challenges and obstacles that must be conquered. My largely pessimistic side shouts how this sucks everyday then I look at my son, remember who I do it for and that pessimism dies quickly. I want to be able to show him that you be whatever you want in this world and teach him that his endless talents come with price tags. Nothing is free in this world, son. Charge them all for your services and write off each charity you provide because after today there is no such thing as a starving artist. If you aren't willing to put yourself out there in the world to get what you want then I don't know what you're praying for.

I wasn't very willing to do that for myself for years. Fear was a friend of mine. Fuck fear. I've got a few more things I'd like to accomplish before I leave planet Earth.

Ain't no losing where I'm coming from
(ain't no going back)
Ain't no looking down
(only looking round)
Where they at?
Where they going when I get here I can't figure out
If you ain't a bank teller nigga what'cha talking bout?
Telling it for years they been boring us ignoring us
My climb to the top will be glorious
Viktorious

SIDE A:
2. what?! where am I?
#nowplaying: Nine Inch Nails - Everyday Is Exactly The Same; Korn - Somebody, Someone

Trees.
Houses.
Trees.
Houses.
Boredom.
Trees.
Houses.
Trees.
Trees.
Boredom.
Boredom.
Boredom.

Once upon a time, Suburbia was a coveted place to live. It's removed from the detritus that is urban city living but also far enough away from rural country living. I think I hate it here. I needed to find something to do with myself instead of repeating that mantra. It makes me believe this is what purgatory must feel like because everyday is exactly the same. Everything is exactly the same. And everyone is exactly the same. Just houses and parked cars. The silence of a residential neighborhood can become deafening over time.

After getting readjusted to being home again, I found myself falling into an everyday routine. Every morning I get the boy and myself ready for school, feed him and take him to daycare. When the day is over, I come home, get dinner ready then pick him up and we'll play until bath time then off to bed around 9pm. It's not glamorous but every time he looks up at me with grinning smiles, I begin to think that moving home wasn't such a bad idea after all. *I gotta get over myself* is my new mantra. But the everyday routine wore itself out and I found myself back at square one: *bored*. My grandmother often says that if you're bored then you're boring. Fuck that. I never want to be boring. No one should want to be boring. However, how can I entertain myself while waiting in purgatory for my next adventure?

I started by learning about my family and returning to a hobby I loved before I left home for college: cooking. I raised my boy to eat adult food because I can't stand a man with a child's palette. He eats almost everything we eat which makes cooking a bit of an exciting adventure and a daunting task when I'm exhausted. During these times of testing new recipes on a toddler, my grandmother would share stories about her family, the things she grew up eating and the trials they went through as African-Americans. Her stories became fascinating because I just never knew facts like how they owned their own grocery store and set up a community medical fund for black people to be able to get medical help. They influenced me to think about life from her point of view and her life's journey. The journey a family takes can provide the strangest sense of confidence that one needs to become an outstanding artist. You begin to analyze things through a different veil because now you're not only representing who you are but where you come from. Your journey becomes inserted into their journeys like a snowball rolling down a hill getting bigger and bigger. We don't know if or when it will break or at all. It just keeps going like you and I.

My conclusion after these talks about the things her family used to do and say was that I was proud to be a part of her family and equally proud to be Southern. That boredom began to fade away with each conversation we had. That everyday routine became appealing again because I began to feel a sense of purpose versus feeling nothing at all. I began thinking about how much Southern black culture has influenced my identity and the way I think even though I am a child of the 21st century which makes me post-Civil Rights. I've lived in the American South my entire life and know nothing else. My language and mannerisms are a prime reflection of living here and I wish to never change who I am ever again. There's nothing like the ungodly humidity during the summer and the almost freezing colds of the winter. To hear the twang of an accent in someone's voice is as exciting as meeting a well-dressed stranger from foreign lands. Yes, the history here is an ugly one but in between the lines are celebrations of food and fellowship that bring us all together at the end of day. I just wish the fellowship part happened more often because that is a reflection of our humanity as people. And I have yet to find someone who doesn't like the sight and smells of Southern food. It's the thing that binds us to our culture.

Southern culture has some of the strongest dualities I have ever seen in my life. Light vs. Dark. Saint vs. Sinner. Black vs. White. City vs. Country even though the whole damn world is country. For every church you see in the light there's always a juke joint, strip club or porn establishment hiding in the dark. For every person that is trying to create a new concept of what it means to be Southern there's always someone to remind you of the extreme racism, prejudice and bigotry. Someone to keep people closed-minded. Someone who wishes for "old times" when opportunity was withheld often from people of color. Homosexuality may even be *prayed away* and never talked about again. That part is ridiculous and often comes from someone who is only conservative to the public. It's also not representative of the entire Southern region's political and religious beliefs. However, when you find an oasis like Atlanta, Charleston, Charlotte, Miami,

New Orleans and other cities I haven't visited yet, you stay there for more than deliciously fattening food and humid, wet weather.

Our culture is perceived as a slow one when compared to international metropolitans like New York, Chicago and Los Angeles, yet we enjoy it that way. I would much rather stop for a conversation or to literally smell some roses than to feel rushed all day long. You need time to think about your next moves hence why coming back home was probably the best idea I've had in two years. I needed this time to think in a place that was quiet and clear enough that I can see the stars at night instead of thick air pollution. I needed to decompress from all the bullshit I caused for myself. Think of Waiting to Exhale without the *angry at black men* part. Being home has helped me to become a better mother, cook, writer and artist. There aren't any noises to interfere with my ability to think. Except for my grandmother moving about at 4am. God! That woman gets up so early.

And now I do, too. Well, not really because I don't get up *that* early. Only early enough to get a grip on the day's activities without hideous hangovers from too much cheap beer and whiskey. I can hear the birds chirping while looking at groups of deer cross suburban streets. There aren't any sirens from police cars or fire trucks buzzing down that same street. Every once in a while a car zooms past quietly because someone is on his or her way to work. There are no trains nearby making screeching sounds as it comes to a stop to pick up passengers. Just silence and nature.

As I pull drags of that first cigarette of morning, I figure out what to do with my day, my life. I make my thoughts concrete and organize one of the biggest "to-do" lists of my life. It looks a lot like this:

1. Be a better person in the world
2. Be a true artist and writer
3. Be a great mother
4. Get your shit together (finances, health/car insurance, the boring/responsible adult stuff)
5. Remember to breathe and don't freak out

That last bit is the hardest. I might be a little masochistic because I like freaking out. It gives a sort of high that can't be achieved with illegal drugs. However, it's unnecessary and wastes much needed time. I don't have time to waste because I really want to take over the world.

I'm not trying to stay in suburgatory forever. I'm going to get out through Heaven or Hell. I've been through Hell once before and I'm not trying to do it again.

SIDE A:
3. alone in the dark at 2am
#nowplaying: FKA twigs - Papi Pacify; XXYYXX - Alone, About You, Breeze & Witching Hour; Beyonce & Andre 3000 - Back to Black
#nowreading: Neil Gaiman - American Gods, Anansi Boys & The Sandman Chronicles: Preludes and Nocturnes

It's 2am. I put my headphones on while keeping an ear out for anyone who may awaken abruptly in the middle of the night. I've had one too many beers in this house tonight and it's that perfect twilight hour to play pretend. The headphones will muffle any noise from the music I've got blasting into my drunken soul. I'm getting a chance to kick off my shoes and be whoever I chose to be. No one can see or hear me. I can act out any scenario and make this lounging den my stage. My responsibilities have multiplied tenfold since the birth of my son and I desperately seek a moment or two to be outlandishly strange and alone. Now that I'm no longer alone, I fiend for it like heroin to an addict. Most people say they hate it. I love it within reason. Too much of it and invisible voices start talking to you. Too little of it and you can't think clearly for yourself. I have no reason to think at this moment because I want to feel like I've jumped off the edge of mountain into another dimension where I am a star high up in the heavens. Somehow I've rationalized that I can get this feeling by drinking too much and acting out my version of Beyonce's Partition video.

I just tripped over my feet trying to be sexy.

no crown, no title: a mixtape of tho(ugh)ts

Change songs. I'm bored with Beyonce. Look at the curves I can make while dancing in the mirror. Let me take my hair down and touch it. Make it messy from running my fingers through clumps and strands. I can touch my body without anyone making a whistling noise or gawking at me making my vibe uncomfortable.

Neck.
Shoulders.
Breasts.
Stomach.
Waist.
Hips.
Thighs.
Legs.
All in that order.

I am not myself at this moment. I am a dream that I pretend to be in order to keep my sanity. I am not a porn star. I am not a light-skinned girl in a music video. I am not a stripper. Even though I pretend to be. I am nothing more than an exotic dream. And somewhere in that dream I find my freedom to be whoever I want to be. Daylight commands that I am to be a responsible woman and mother who cares for her son. When night comes, I am to be asleep in order to be well-rested for the next day so I can repeat the same routine. But not tonight. I want to just break free for a moment. Hell, I know I'm gonna pay for it in the morning with a beating head and gurgling stomach because who doesn't like to get lost in dancing? There's so much that goes through my head on a daily basis. Filter after filter in order to process the loads of information that we, as humans, take in on a daily basis. Seeing with my eyes, listening with my ears, thinking with my brain and touching with my hands. I drunkenly think to myself "Death to authority and preconceived notions!" because in this moment, this witching hour I am only rebelling against the responsibility I've placed upon myself. I've checked out and started moving to the beat.

Play Beyonce & Andre 3000 on repeat for the next 30 minutes.

I begin imagining about visuals of creatures that I would love to create. It doesn't matter to me if they move or rest inside white picture frames. The gods and monsters I create through collage come to life and dance with me in the dark. Words I didn't have before come flowing out like water breaking loose on land. I begin thinking about what I wish I had made or said at moments in time. Those thoughts fade to black and the monsters come back. I can see their brightly colored wings expand in this den. It is no longer a den but the cosmos above. In here and at this hour, my imagination can finally exceed the boundaries placed upon me. I am the supreme king of my dreams because they give me comfort unlike anything made on Earth. I step on heavenly clouds while tripping balls with God. I am a creator. And this is my playground because as an artist, it is very important to have these types of moments to yourself. A moment where your mind can run free in order to create worlds upon worlds of your choosing.

It's these kinds of thoughts that make the ability to daydream rather important. One day while I was sitting in a black-owned business in Charlotte, I commented about how much I hate daydreams because I haven't achieved them yet. The owner, a young woman named Davita, changed my mind by simply stately that they are actually a very good thing because they give you a chance to be free. Within seconds, my mind recalled a passage from Neil Gaiman's The Sandman Chronicles, in particular, Preludes and Nocturnes. Gaiman's version of the Sandman had to travel to Hell to retrieve artifacts that belonged to him. After playing and winning a game with Beezlebub, Lucifer Morningstar (the Devil) commented on how much more powerful he is than the Sandman and couldn't wait to keep him down to Hell. The Sandman scoffed at the idea of the Devil being more powerful than him. His reply back to him questioned what would Hell be like if there were no dreams? The Sandman soon left to continue on his journey to collect the rest of his artifacts.

My mind was blown and I soon rescinded my hate for daydreaming. We all do it. It's what fuels us to move on to bigger and better things. If we didn't have the ability to dream... I don't know what we would do as humans. The world would be a much different place and I believe we'd really be functioning like robots. These emotionless creatures walking about with no ability to be moved by the things we see, say and do. I believe that part of the job of being an artist is to bring dreams to life through the power of creation. I don't much care if you use words, pencils, paints or photography. Ideas begin as dreams. Once we decide to implement the idea, it transforms into a concept and begins to bloom into reality. The end result is something that is concrete like a poem, essay, drawings, painting, photo shoot or all of the above. Now, will viewers see the artist's dream the way the artist does? Sadly, no. But they will walk away with an experience that if received well will change their lives forever or give them something good to think about. It always either this or that.

For example, when I make my work, I think about all of my favorite mythological tales of creation from across the globe. I put myself in the mind of what it would take to create something that has never been seen before and how that something will affect my viewers. I decide that I want to empower what I see, what I am frequently blasted with through conventional media. For me, when I see women that look like me, I find that my reflection is overly exoticized, hypersexualized and used like a sex toy. My reflection is rendered powerless or villainous because of my role as a sexualized woman. This is not me in reality. These are women on television, movies and the internet. Spaces where the idea of simulation runs free becoming simulacra into reality. Women similar to me begin to believe they must be like these simulated women. Other women believe they should not be. Both leave no room for the woman who embraces her sensuality and sexuality. I make my work for that woman. The woman who chooses to no longer be affected by these images. The women who pursues self-empowerment yet understands the self-conscious nature of being human. She reverses the power totem pole upside down because power is not a male-centered concept for her. She knows that power has been in the palm of her hands her entire life.

These are the things I think about while drunk and alone very late at night. By this hour, I'm pantless staring at my legs noticing the light cast upon them from the flicker of the television. I should probably go to bed but I want to hear just one more song. I hope I can remember these thoughts in the morning.

SIDE A:
4. on being an artist
#nowplaying: Kendrick Lamar - Bitch, Don't Kill My Vibe & Money Trees; TV On The Radio - Wolf Like Me & Staring At The Sun

Imagine waking up in a blank zone. You are the king of the throne. Everything you touch turns into gold, red, green or blue. You take those colors and begin forming shapes which you then form into figures. Your fingertips spark life into your figures. They listen to you. They're at your command. They belong to you. You begin filling in details transforming this zone into a world no one has ever explored. Maybe you have flora. Maybe there is fauna. Maybe you create dark skies and fill your world with scary, bloodthirsty monsters that wreck havoc throughout the heavens and Earth. It all feels so very real. Very, very real.

But it's all in your mind.

This is your imagination because you are an artist.

What does it take to be an artist? It's a little more than drawing on a sheet of paper or dabbing a paintbrush into some paint. It takes some thought and some creativity wherever the hell that shit comes from. When you're a child, you're introduced to it through drawing. You become addicted instantly if it's really your thing. Every minute of your childhood is spent trying to draw everything that you see. Flowers, bottles, landscapes, cityscapes, everything.

A blank white sheet of paper can become instantly filled from corner to corner. Maybe there's a figure that needs to be grounded or a line that changes directions every so often. Then you grow up and realize you really want to be an artist. Something that has taken me over 10 years to define and I've learned that it's damn near anything.

Most people expect for me to be a painter when I mention that I am an artist. I hate painting. I have no control over the medium. Every artist is not a fucking painter therefore stop expecting us to be. I don't sit around drawing little sketches nor do I get joy from setting up an easel to paint. There's just more to art than that. What makes me an artist is more about thought process than actual painting and drawing. Those are acquired skills because someone can teach you how to draw and paint. Artists, I believe, are naturally born. Some people come into this world as such while circumstances can create an artist. One of my favorite sayings is *every artist has some sort of a fucked up childhood*. Define that part as you will. Some folks have horrific experiences growing up but find the strength to grow past them. In my case, I was quite lonely and had the television as a best friend because I was too shy to make real friends. As my skills grew so did the attention I received and I fell in love with it. I haven't been able to let it go as I've gotten older. I'm permanently stuck in the *Look what I made, Mom* stage of life. Every artist is different when given a sheet of paper to fill because we all have a different story to tell. The human experience is varied. If we lived the same lives, I believe that we'd be a rather boring group of people.

Recently, I was at an event that showcased some young painters from North Carolina. Two of them, Wesley and Ghost, were pretty dope while rest were pretty bad. The people that attended clearly enjoyed being in the presence of these creative people. Many expressed themselves through their attire hoping to stand out in the crowd. Others were standing around observing the artists paint new dreams on canvas. There is an invisible transmission of energy passing back and forth. The crowd unknowingly feeding into the egos of the artists and the artists giving the crowd what they want by expressing their creativity in front of them. It's quite voyeuristic now that I think about it. They want to bask in our presences and watch as we change the atmosphere into something sensual. Wesley, a painter, took a young lady's selfie from Instagram and transformed it into an expressive portrait complete with bright neon orange accents. The young woman has now attained a new level of beauty. As his painting was heading toward near completion, a small crowd began to gather around him to watch him. Someone took a picture. I'm sure it was posted to Instagram that same hour of the evening.

I honestly can't begin to tell you why we love what we do. We've all done this for so long that it feels innate to be creative. Something about life moves you in such a way to express yourself through the tips of your fingers. Some folk choose to do it musically, some through sculpting and others through photography. Some creative expression is beautiful and moving, some will make you introspective and some will be graphically horrific. After all these years, art is still subjective as fuck and only those that command its history will accept it as a part of the Western arts canon. Those people miss out on the great parts of being an artist and I currently do not have the power to change that. (Yet.)

All I can do with the power that I have now is let you know who are the dopest artists in whatever town or city I pass through. It doesn't take much to know either. Many artists have a stank (also known as aura or vibe) lingering around them. When I see this, I instantly have to check them out. I start with a barrage of questions before I let them know I make work as well.

Who are you?
What do you do (or Is this your work)?
Why do you do this?
Can you tell me about it?

Stay quiet and let them speak. Don't interrupt anymore.

For me, it doesn't matter if the artist is academically trained or not. What matters is if this person studies their craft, practices their craft and skillfully expands on their craft. We live in an age where information is right at our fingertips. You can learn whatever you want to learn at any given time. Art doesn't have room for excuses on improvement. For example, some of my favorite "self-taught" artists are from Atlanta. Chilly-O, a photographer and videographer, takes beautiful portraits of black skaters and bikers in the city as well as moody fashion photography portraits. He knows exactly what he is looking for when he shoots, can describe to you his reason behind the lighting in his images and the technical details he used to create his shots. And no, he didn't go to a fancy art school to learn how to do these things. Photography became a way to express himself and from there he took control by learning more about his craft.

Another person I highly regard is Miya Bailey, an Atlanta-based tattoo artist. He briefly attended Art Institute of Atlanta and like many students walked away before completion. In the time that I've known him, I've seen his illustrations develop into an identifiably bold and graphic style with hints of Ethiopian art styles. He sources from all over the place in terms of inspiration but when you get down to the nitty gritty of his work, the line is king. Each line detail must be strong in order to handle the power of the needle used for tattooing and that translates onto paper beautifully. His bright, vibrant and bold color palette is recognizable because he never uses muted colors. When it's time to for him to switch to his personal artistic practices, I believe he enters what I think is an imaginary, wide-open blank space where his images come to life and travel through him from space onto a fabric or skin canvas.

Both of these men are grown men with families. They have bills to pay and mouths to feed. Art cannot be romanticized because the real world is always at their front door knocking. However, art can provide an escape from real world. We need a place to get away even if it's imaginary. Every artist has that kind of space. Inside of it is complete freedom and we can access that space at any given time of the day. It's one of our superpowers. We can attract people, create new realities and escape to our secret lair whenever we need.

I wish I had a secret lair at this very moment. I'd retreat the hell away from these 6th graders and make my monsters eat them as a way to relax at the end of a day of being a substitute.

Damn. I wondered off. Back on track.

To escape is to acknowledge escapism which leads to fantasizing about people, places and things. Known and unknown. Artists retreat often to come face to face with their inspiration. Some artists are just trying to escape what we've been told is the real world. The real world can't possibly be real because too many suffer within its form. When an artist creates, he or she also appears to be antisocial in the real world. He or she appears awkward or socially inept. This isn't true. This person has seen something that no one else can see. The errors of society or the beauty of something that has been deemed savage. An artist questions reality and asks if it is even real at all when their imaginative world appears so real to them. When their world unfolds, it is only then that our audience has the chance to experience the power and excitement of being an artist.

And what a very powerful space that is to be in.

SIDE A:
5. their eyes stopped watching god
#nowwatching: The Signal
#nowreading: The Invisibles by Grant Morrison, From Hell & V for Vendetta by Alan Moore

I lost my marbles in 2009 when I started reading a graphic novella called *The Invisibles* by Grant Morrison. With each page absorbed I could hear what I perceived to be reality falling to the floor, plinking and breaking with every marble dropped. The basis of the story is what if every paranormal, supernatural or conspiracy event were true? What would you do? Who would you run to for help? You'd run to the Invisibles! Cells of people with extraordinary powers fighting against the established powers that be.

Everything that no one ever addresses or is too scared to do so is in those books. Literally, everything.

There are globby aliens that eat people and are held captive levels below Area 51. There are monsters from unknown dimensions that can be accessed through a special mirror and it feeds on people. There are rich men that hunt homeless men, women and children for sport on islands far away because they believe no one will miss them. There is a Voodoo spirit that is a rapper who walks between worlds, sex slaves from the Enlightenment era and a time travelling BDSM historical icon also known as the Marquis de Sade. There's quite a bit of magic inside this omnibus which feels like bombs exploding in your mind at the conclusion of each segment.

At one point, I had to put the novella down for three months to get myself back together and actually finish my grad school matriculation. This only happened because a section about the Voodoo rapper Jim Crow and another about the Marquis really screwed with me and I lost all focus. They were gory, graphic and hitting too close to home for it to be *just* a comic book. I eventually finished the novella, graduated on time and found a shitty job to hold me down until I determined next moves. I didn't have a camera to borrow after I graduated and resorted to collaging to create the images that were beginning to crowd my mind after finishing the books.

Those stories stayed on my mind like echoes in the wind with every waking day I've had since completion. My imagination was active again as I pretended to see crowns and halos on the everyday people I watched while riding on MARTA throughout Atlanta at 5am for my shitty job. Soon I began creating reinterpretations of portraits that highlighted the poor man and woman as righteous saints, kings and queens. They became a metaphor for how I began to see blackness and classism in America. I was seeking to actively change the hierarchies of power. Just like what I experienced reading *The Invisibles*.

By 2010 I left my pissant job for a better position as an arts instructor at a historically black college in middle Georgia. Something that fit me much better than pressing keychains of childrens sports photography. I was much happier teaching young black college students with similar upbringings as me. In the beginning I didn't know exactly what to do with myself but I made a decision that if I was going to tell them that I am an artist then I need to be a working artist while my students worked on their projects. We didn't have the same access to supplies like my graduate school could offer therefore I had to become very creative with our projects and resorted to collaging as something I could do to teach the students the basic elements of art and design. I stopped making my personal work just briefly enough to get a better grasp on education and how to be better prepared for the students. When I am in that arena, nothing is more important to me than them because they have come to me to learn a particular set of skills that I've spent over 10 years studying and continue to do so. I often made my assignments project-based with routinely scheduled research papers on artists and movements.

On class days reserved for studio time, I used to sit back quietly and listen to them talk about whatever subject was on their mind. I rarely policed their conversations unless I felt it was something that was rude or offensive to another group of students. It was during this time that I learned the most about them. I would hear about songs that they like, experiences they had, television shows they watched and their perspective of American culture. Everything was always cool until that point. Some of them had some negative views of life because nothing was available to empower them as young adults. All of their heroes were killed before they were born and none have risen since. They mostly did as they were told with one or two students who believed themselves to be bucking at the system. Many of them allowed the influence of pop culture to takeover their ideas, concepts and beliefs about black culture. It ruled how they viewed relationships, careers and religious beliefs. It was like their eyes were completely covered or masked to what was happening around them.

This began to bother me and when I become bothered I begin to think. And think. And think.

How could this happen? Why is it happening? Who seeks to benefit the most from this type of thinking. When I came to a conclusion, I had made a series of collages that were the most topsy turvy things I had ever created in my life. It contained bits and pieces of the same pop culture elements we had been exposed to such as blinged out rappers, curvaceous exotic strippers and big glossy candy cars as chariots. The cosmos became halos for these unlikely heroistic characters. The eyes were cut out and replaced with non-textured bright colors or bodies of text out of magazines. I had essentially began making a new visual mythology using dirty South (known in this sense as a Southern subculture) archetypes. I used the people and topics my students always referenced and turned them into something else. Something that would allow them to create their own stories because they believed in stories that always referenced them as a side character like a servant to royalty. To me they were royalty no matter how their lives turned out for them.

I began exhibiting the works in shows and museums and realized that many people gravitated to my collages because they saw something in them that awakened them. At that moment, I experienced the power of art, communication and influence. Especially for women of color. Many women would come to me with questions about why I chose to use an exotic dancer or porn star to be a God-like character in my works. By the time I finished prattling about my work, they understood what I understood. Images in popular culture are meant to exploit women no matter how soft and pretty. I could no longer mindlessly flip through glossy magazines without passing judgment on the women photographed. Black and Latino women were always hypersexualized beings while white and Asian women always appeared submissive and innocent. These attributes are not indicative of all women because every woman is different with different perspectives and thoughts. Yet flipping through a magazine one would believe otherwise. I soon expanded my characters to include all kinds of women I would find in magazines because inside those glossy pages, I had the strongest internal conflict over self-esteem and identity.

Our eyes stopped watching God and instead we worship the hypersexiness of popular culture. A simulation of a simulation. Simulacrum cum. Lawd!

Many trick themselves into believing that they can't do anything at all to change the power of big media in the United States. I may not have the power to change everyone but like *The Invisibles* I have the power to change one person at a time using a twisted tale of disgust, oppression, power and desire. In my works, I give power to the powerless. Pawns become kings and whores become queens with purpose. Everybody needs a purpose in life. No one needs to walk around with their eyes covered to tragedies scattered around them disguised as false happiness. My happiness is in my power to define my life. My happiness is in the belief that I am breaking psychological chains from our connections to popular media images that tell us all how to live our lives.

The Invisibles is just a story. *V for Vendetta* is just a story. Both are about our easy willingness to comply at the hands of violence and the people who chose to buck against the system created to maintain order and keep power in the hands of the powerful elites. Aren't you bored of this? I know that I am. I am not a sexual object. I am not Beyonce or a Puerto Rican porn star. And i love both of these women. I don't want to be a housewife to a man that doesn't see me as his equal but as his trophy. I am not a dowry. I am a human. I am a person just like my former and future students. I love where I come from but I don't love what America wishes for me to be. And I am changing it the best way I know how.

Through the power of art and communication.

SIDE B:
6. a letter to Beyonce and Anthony Bourdain
#nowplaying: Beyonce (the whole self-titled album)
#nowwatching: Parts Unknown

Dear Beyonce and Anthony Bourdain,

The two of you appear to have nothing in common on the surface. One is an international pop singer married to an equally famous rapper. The other is a former chef, writer and host to the Emmy and James Beard Award winning show, *Parts Unknown*. One of you recently went vegan. The other doesn't like vegan unless he dines in India or with Yotem Ottolenghi. To others, you may seem worlds apart but to me you are the best representations of how my mind works. I write you this fictitious letter not as a fan but as an intellectual defending how to two of you make sense to me because my inspiration isn't solely driven by art alone. If they were, I'd probably be as boring as those deeply involved in the arts. My blinders would be set to regard only what I have been trained to learn about art via academia. That represents a life not worth living. I'm fueled by my experiences growing up in North Carolina. My fantasies are influenced by pop culture. My knowledge was created by untangling the mess that is history using rebellious voices not inside my head. Both of you have been playing in the background of my life as I watched you perform only on television. One of you can sing your heart to world without it feeling contrived. The other exposed millions of American audiences to the world via food travels without it feeling contrived as well. The both of your perspectives are influential and I turned y'all into muses for how I interpret the world in front of me.

These next thoughts go out to y'all.

To M. Bourdain -

What I appreciate most from someone like you is your ability to articulate issues regarding global cultures and societies. I was able to feel a connection once I moved past ogling these strange world dishes you were eating and began listening to your narrations about why you chose to visit a particular country or city. When I read your writings, I imagine you narrating your adventures in a Fear and Loathing kind of way. They have influenced the way that I write as your words were equally influenced by the words of Hunter Thompson.

We are not kindred spirits. We never will be. But I can always understand a man who is a former rebellious kid and punk rock enthusiast because those qualities are within me. What I ultimately learn from you is the remembrance that writing is such a powerful source of intellectual activism and to live life the best way we know how. By just fucking living it. By asking questions and investigating things that we don't know. What is life if we allow ourselves bow down to authority living like brainwashed pawns? That is not a life at all. That is a neverending hell. One I cannot possibly live in.

Once upon a time, you were at your lowest of low. Many people in the world have been in similar situations having chains of self-doubt holding them down and escaping through whatever drug suits their fancy. Only few have been able to really crawl their way out and start over. Even fewer get a chance to start their lives over again. It is rare that they achieve the possibilities that you have. It takes pure drive from the bottom of your insides to the top of your soul to get to where you are. I seek the same power within myself.

Here's to you, Anthony Bourdain. You are one of my Umis and you shine your dusty, flickering light for all the world to see. Your voice seems to always tell it how you feel and your memories didn't forget the people you met along the way. You aren't another chef crush but truly a muse because of how you chose to analyze the world through your favorite tools of trade: food, drinks and good conversation. The combination of these three things are the backbones for digging deeply into any topic deemed too controversial to discuss over any proper dinner.

When speaking of complex issues regarding classism, identity, racism, religion and sexism, one should feel the need to be in an improper environment. Or an environment that has been deemed improper by the elite status quo. When you are in such place, you humble yourself to the voices of the people you are interviewing. You're a walking relic of writers before you that didn't see the world as this happy suburban white place. You're a observational fly on the wall like Tom Wolfe and emotional like Charles Bukowski and Jack Kerouac. So am I. When I write, I seek to inform, engage and enlighten with humor and sarcasm. Unlike you, I prefer to write with a passion like Zora Neale Hurston and James Baldwin because they are me and I am them. They are more powerful in written word than those I referenced for you yet everyone I've named has changed the course of American culture at some point in our shared history.

For years I've watched you become your own investigator with *Why?* as your leader. You opened up audiences to experience what isn't an establishment of Western influence. I wish I could explore the world too, instead of viewing it from television sets and the internet. Luckily, for those of us that can't just up and go to places like Brazil, South Africa or Thailand, we appreciate you giving us a ground view of what it would be like to be there and the kinds of things we could possibly experience instead of hiding behind resort walls. Possibly another space that many of us will never be able to walk through. I often criticize big media for holding too much power over audiences but I can't deny moments when it is great and entertaining like your show. For every episode that I've watched, I haven't seen anyone from around the world being exploited for who they are. They are treated and regarded with a level of respect that every human deserves. You make it appear that there is no such thing as savages to the civilized world.

Your honesty is refreshing in world where lies are so real that they are the truth to so many believers. You remind us that seeing and experiencing for ourselves is better than believing anything ZPZ Productions could produce for CNN. In your works, I realize that the whole world damn world is country, deals with bullshit government politics, celebrates their culture as much as I celebrate mine and seems to really love any form of chicken and rice. It's because of you that I want to break bread with as many people of the world as I can before I die. Only then will I have truly lived a life fulfilled and I don't care if it is only in the city that I live in or globe trotting as the artist and writer that I am.

Thank you.

To Beyonce -

Unlike entertainers that I loved before you, you are the only one I've experienced the ability to grow older with. When you were on Star Search with Girls Tyme, I probably caught that episode after Saturday morning cartoons. By the time Destiny's Child was beginning to become a huge deal, I ignored you, except for *Jumpin' Jumpin'* and *Say My Name*, because I refused to relate to the music. I had never dealt with any kind of heartbreak and had not bloomed into my own femininity yet. That journey was just starting to begin and I stayed pretty critically harsh of you until I heard *B'Day*. Something snapped inside of me when I heard that album. When I encountered it, I instantly connected with it because I could understand the feminine experience throughout the album. I had explored and played with different sides of myself before that point. Going through the same phase every 19 and 20-something young girl goes through by wearing clothes too revealing and putting on too much make up thinking I was grown because I was no longer in my grandmother's house. I felt that I was nerdy enough and needed to express myself to be like an attractive girl I had seen in a music video but instead hid behind the veil that if I looked a certain way then some certain guy would actually be attracted to me. Both times, during *Dangerously In Love* and *B'Day*, I was wrong and these falsehoods are what hurt my feelings most than what any guy had done to me.

Every video released for *B'Day* became of representation of things I was feeling and images that I loved. I realized at that point that I couldn't talk shit about anything Beyonce related because I had become a fan. Then there was *Sasha Fierce*. I wasn't for that because at that moment you weren't singing to me. It went against the relationship I had with *B'Day*. Then you wooed me back with *4* through our love for pop culture and the Dirty South. You were pregnant with Blue and realized that girls really run the world because without us… how would people really get here? A sneakily simple question with some very complex answers that only a woman can answer. And then came *BEYONCE*, the self-titled album that shitted on any and everything we knew about you. You made us fall in love with you again because me and every girl we know in our 30-something age felt the *fuck it* that drips all over and throughout that album.

I didn't need to recognize that you're an adult because I already knew that. What I recognized was that it reminded me of the things women go through and the thoughts we have. I believe that in this current century, we are dealing with the creation of a new form of woman. What has been described as femininity is finally coming to a close. No longer do some women want to plan their lives to revolve around a man and marriage. I have my own life with the power of being a mother. Some will never know that power because the power of a mother has been downplayed and exaggerated for laughs in the name of entertainment or my personal hated that "moms don't do those things because they are moms." That's called denial of happiness when that's all you have to really achieve in this life.

I write to you not because you're a top paid entertainer, not because you sing way better than most and not because you have a huge team of people behind you helping to drive you success. I write to you because within that self-titled visual album there is a song and video for where I stand as a young woman. The diversity of the album reflects my diversity. If I were to have a significant other, my fantasies of our sexual life would play out like *Partition* and *Blow*. If I just want to rock out with my homies, my fantasies would play out like *Haunted, XO* and *Superpower*. However, buried within *Flawless* is something that is very key to my letter for you.

The feminism speech by Chimamanda Ngozi Adiche brings our worlds into collision. Add that with *Pretty Hurts* and the world has a bold example of what it means to a woman. We are set up to believe in notions of femininity that hurt us in the long run. There is no sensual freedom or intellectual prowess. A woman is not my competition and a man is not my enemy. Socialized patriarchal behavior has changed the relationship dynamics of men and women so much that it takes learning feminism to unravel the damage. We are supposed to live our lives scared, helpless and in need of a man to protect us. Prince Charming doesn't exist and bitch, I know you agree with me. Fuck all that when I can live my life by writing my own story. Fuck trying to be like the stories written before me. I am not Eve.

Many still think a woman's mouth should be stapled closed and that we only follows the orders of men. To them, there is no such thing as equality. It is a dream deferred or entertaining dinner conversation that doesn't deserve action. If we act upon teaching women to attain self-power, independence and financial freedom then we are outcasted, believed to be crazy or put in a box away from the ability to influence. How much power does a woman really have if everything that makes her a woman is taught to be so contained? Numerous outcasted women paved a laborious path before you in order for you to become that woman that you are today. What is shitty for them compared to you is that they do not have the international platform that you have. What if these women's voices were heard as loudly as yours? Think of how many people you have introduced Adiche to by simply putting her in the middle of song that's about every girl waking up believing that she is flawless? If certain women missed it the first time, in due time they will seek the speaker and more knowledge about her out.

My words to you are just as special as the ones I had for Monsieur Bourdain. He is the catalyst for these words I have for you by making me examine what I have to say about your music. I have no need to demonize you like bell hooks because I do not believe you to be a harm to young girls. I think we need to fully recognize that having only entertainers as role models for young girls and women is ridiculous because there are so many different kinds of men and women that deserve to be regarded as role models. The only way any of us are to ever meet them is if we get off the couch and explore our world. That is ultimately what you and Bourdain have in common that I love. No experience from anyone is overlooked. The only way some of the videos for *BEYONCE* could have been successful is if you enjoyed being on the ground with the people around you because honestly until the day you die, you'll never really be able to experience what it is like to walk out into a street and eat local fare without a crowd forming within 5 minutes or less of you leaving a hotel. I have that advantage over you and so does Bourdain. But you have the power to meet and be around the powerful people of this world. It is my hopes that you never let your on-the-ground experiences go unnoticed in their presence because I know you have the power to change whomever you encounter. Look at me. I've just completed a gushy, intellectual, fictitious fan letter to you.

C'est la vie tho.

Love,
Carla

SIDE B:
7. a culture of ratchetry
#nowplaying: Ying Yang Twins - Whistle While You Twerk; Hot Boyz - I Need a Hot Girl; DJ Snake feat. Lil Jon - Turn Down For What?!

As the internet began rolling into more houses nationwide since the late 90s and the rise of our present vehicle of internet access through smartphones and tablets, everybody's sex game and language has changed for better and worse. During all of this, the strip club became elevated to popular status and is no longer viewed as a seedy environment with girls at the end of their social lifelines dancing for lonely, desperate men. You can now find any man and woman in this space from closet freak soccer moms to unorthodox businessmen solidifying contracts. I blame the Sopranos for this jolt in strip club popularity. I can also blame rap music culture for this rise as well but why? You may find me in a skin club in Atlanta drawing girls on my smartphone while drinking beer. Let's not be hypocritical here.

Let's face it. Sex sells and being ratchet is the new cool. All of this didn't suddenly begin with former Disney stars like Britney Spears and Miley Cyrus either. Nor is it solely a product of black America. I wish for these notions to die. It's something that has always existed underneath the constructed ideal that America is a puritanical society. That's a surface level thought. A projection of what one wishes to see and believe. Humans are naturally curious of each others bodies when shared attraction comes into play. We have aggrandized sexuality through internet usage by making pornography free to viewers then use it's influence on how we interact with popular movies & music. We worship sex more than Jesus (if you even worship him at all). We're obsessed with it. There's a bit of ratchet in everyone. Thanks to pop culture, we live in a culture of ratchetry.

RATCHET (adj.) - a term for someone who is either 1. a whore; 2. dirty/nasty; 3. ghetto as HELL; 4. being annoying; 5. busted. Originally known (and still known) as a socket wrench tool. A nation of tools.

Doesn't that definition sound like some bullshit? If you just agreed then we agree. We live in a culture of bullshit. We condemn the dirty whore in public but wish to be her behind close doors and offer billions in American dollars to watch her sexually disgrace herself all the time. That's backwards as hell. We publicly admonish a black girl with colorful weave twerking in Wal-Mart but celebrate a white girl with colorful hair doing the same thing. That's also backwards as hell. Both are being ratchet and participating in ratchet actions. I find no difference between the two.

I've learned that sex controls many everyday behaviors for a lot of people. People allow it to control their outer appearance in the name of sexual attraction. It controls our verbal and nonverbal communication when we speak and touch. Lastly, it controls how we think and choose to interact with the living world. That last bit is insane to me. I believe that's what happens when you deem one sex inferior to another sex. For example, when men decided to rule the world, women became second and are viewed as being inferior therefore anyone possessing feminine qualities is viewed as an inferior human being. Add racist and classist notions to that belief then sprinkle in identity and responsibility politics and you'll end up with a clusterfuck that seems difficult to untangle. Luckily and thankfully, there are many people, including myself, interested in untangling this awful social mess.

With the rise of the millenials, there are a few things culturally happening right now that need discussion. First, language as a powerful tool is being redefined as we speak and changing how we interact with the world. Third wave feminists and social activists are at the forefront of this mission by battling male-centered language which has influenced our human communication and are de-centering those that have been marginalized. The concepts of acceptance and understanding are being integrated into everyday language which can be powerful. We live in a world where people are trying desperately to define their individual identity. Tradition appears as if it is dying but it hasn't. For example, international women's rights is only proper if we regard the different types of women on this Earth with respect to their cultures. Within these groups of women are different identities. No one is the same as the next yet all women deal with the same lack of rights from the East to the West. In nearly every society across the globe, there is a gap between men and women in terms of education, pay, property ownership and civil rights. In the United States, more women are becoming educated but still lack income inequalities compared to men. But why? My guess is patriarchal power still rules over financial independence. Lil Kim told me a long time ago that first, you get the money, then you get the power and then you get the respect. She never really told me how besides showing me her body and repeating sexualized rap verses that someone else wrote. *Allegedly*.

On the surface, it seems that a woman can get naked in a club and shake her body parts for hundreds to thousands of dollars per night or make a skin flick in 30 minutes for the same amount. The cost? Over time, such a lifestyle changes that woman's psychology and her outlook on life. There will be many great nights and very bad *us vs. them* nights. I've seen in it in the eyes of many girls over and over again. With every adversity against women, how could a woman start her adult life here? For some it really is about survival for themselves and their children. For some it really is about paying for education when there is no one to help you get through college which can be very expensive. Sometimes, these women move on allowing it to be a part of her ratchet past. It happens. However, popular culture will allow you to believe these women are winning because of their sexual independence. If you sacrifice some skin via strip club, become an internet porn model or "accidentally" drop a sex tape then you will gain the financial independence you seek, girl. Nope because hidden from you are the growing numbers of sexual assault and rape cases that happen to these women. Just be a little ratchet for fun, girl. The world loves to watch you, girl. But if you participate in this behavior then you deserve what you get, girl.

That is so dangerous, girl. How did you fall into this simulated trap, girl? We perceive that it is all right to participate in this type of sexual activity because of the number of easily accessible images, moving and still, on the internet. Why send a sexy image to someone that you like? I don't know. I can't look down on any man or woman that does because I've done it myself. We all love to feel wanted by someone. We love to tease and tantalize that somebody as well. I'm just not sure if the entire world needs to know. Like I said, we love being ratchet but look down on being ratchet all at once. We judge others if they aren't ratchet at all and they judge us right back. What right do we have to judge people and their sexual behaviors?

What I can agree with is sexual respectability. Sexuality can be great to watch, exciting to explore and thrilling to experiment. Respectability not in the sense of looking like a Trojan condom commercial where two people are getting on and a mysterious voice meant to mock your conscience shows up to suggest using one. But in the sense that if I'm in the park with my child and you're in the park with your significant other, you're respectable enough to not fuck right there in front of my child. Let him keep him innocence and spare me of disgust. Respect that some people are sensitive to certain sexual behaviors. The public doesn't want to hear about sexual escapades of the previous night while riding public transportation with you. It's not that you can't talk about it with your friends but even I abhor hearing about things like that so very loudly in not so very wide open spaces. It's weird and invasive of my personal space. No one should say that you can't participate in some weird sexual activity and no one should dictate what kind of sexual activity you should participate in. *(Sidenote: I do not condone sexual activity with children, animals or dead people. Two of those things are just fucking weird and the other is flat out dead wrong. But it's okay to have an adult piss on you, shit on you and/or throw beans on you then fuck you. I'm just saying.)*

If we didn't participate in some form of ratchet behavior or another then how would humans get here? By forcing a man and woman to mate against their own will? That has happened plenty of times throughout human history and the outcomes of those families haven't been too pretty. Should we control sexual interactions between humans? Tricky question with an even trickier answer but no, we can't do that either because we would end up back at the beginning argument about women's rights. Let us also include that we would eventually transition into gay and transgender rights if you're talking to me.

The only conclusion I can think of is that our answers may really be within feminism. For years, I've tried to lean away from believing that feminism can save our social responsibilities as humans but I've come to be wrong. I still have my issues with it because I honestly do not like being tagged along with a group of people. But when I open my eyes to the bigger picture of what's happening around me, what's happening to people like me and see the strength of what happens when a group of people seek social change, I can't help but agree that within feminism can we really be set free. Women and men are taught to be competitive with one another and use their sexual prowess to gain power in the world when it doesn't have to be that way. You don't have to be what you see of women and men in popular movies, music and television in order to be seen as sexy, beautiful or daring. It's your mindset that makes you sexy, beautiful and daring. So what if you like being a little ratchet with your friends on the weekends? So what if you like being ratchet in the bedroom for your significant other? So what if your favorite sexual fetish is seen as ratchet?

We're all a little ratchet in some way. I'm just here to call out the bullshit when ratchetry gets judged, compartmentalized and/or goes awry because somewhere in America, your mom is twerking with her friends or for a nigga she's fucking.

SIDE B:
8. in defense of niggadom
#nowplaying: Young Jeezy - Lose My Mind; Lil Jon and the Eastside Boys feat. Ludacris & Chyna White - Bia Bia; Webbie - Come Here Bitch

Not many folk realize where niggas come from. Is it solely a black thing? I don't think I'm so sure anymore. Sitting on a train in New York or riding a bus in Los Angeles will expose you to different kinds of people who utilize the word as if they've been called a nigga their entire life. It's rather weird and very disconcerting because most folk fall into the culture of niggadom through hip-hop/rap music. They never realize that if you deal with niggas, you become a nigga. They are a special group of people created by American classism and racism. They have transformed parts of slavery's horrific ugliness into a visual culture that is now strongly ingrained in global popular culture. However, the power of the nigga is still removed from him and her. Their bodies are still not their own. Their actual voices are rarely heard. When they protest, no one listens. When they celebrate, everybody wants to join in becoming the butt of many jokes.

As I study art and culture, I get a chance to reflect on history past, the present moment and the future to come. In terms of black bodies, there is a vast split in the art world. Its proper folk are in a deep love affair with fetishizing the black body over and over again. They seem to always praise works by artists of color that remind us over and over again of the institutionalized oppression of slavery with slave images. See *12 Years A Slave* as an award-winning example. It's a prime artistic reinforcement that we are subordinate people that are used to being treated subhuman. At that point, I begin to wonder about the influence of power and how we choose to interpret power through a post-colonialist lens. All I can ever see is how whiteness has almost washed away blackness in the professional art world. I'm not saying we must be and/or act like niggas but the spectrum of blackness is rarely ever present. If your accent is too thick or you choose to communicate in a different version of the English language then those things are looked down upon. If your voice is too broad and powerful, you'll be viewed as scary. If you're tattooed all over then you've been in a gang and possibly dangerous. To express the individual blackness that is you appears to be a cardinal sin but this is the art world. It wasn't established for me or you when we decided we wanted to be a part of it.

It broke my heart when I realized those things as an observer and participant. The negro is in a constant state of spectacle so much that in my mind I believe Guy Debord was truly referencing people of color. In this section, I paired together my criticisms of Kara Walker's A Subtlety installation and Jay-Z shooting *Picasso Baby* in Pace Gallery because the two topics reflect the ongoing struggling nature of blackness in America. As I publicly disagreed with Walker's installation, I had more people telling me that I was wrong for disliking a big white powdered sugar mammy. The negress was the spectacle but the naysayers never understand that.

Guess what you motherfuckers... Fuck Mammy.

No Subtlety: A Grotesque Understanding of A Marvelous Sugar Baby

What more can possibly be said about Kara Walker? She is known as the youngest MacArthur "genius" as well as the youngest artist to receive a retrospective in the Metropolitan

Museum of Art in New York. As for her work, her Antebellum paper silhouettes compel you to look and keep looking because of the grotesque and violent details. It makes you question yourself as you see black mammies and picaninnies get their revenge on former masters and mistresses by raping them with kitchen utensils, taking shits in their modest presence or allowing black bodies to combine into ghastly monsters. You begin to wonder why you like it as you walk around her exhibitions because after a while you're a little disturbed by the racially charged content.

Recently, Creative Time NYC and Kara Walker collaborated on a project to be housed inside of an old Domino Sugar Plant in Brooklyn, New York. As with the rest of Brooklyn's gentrification, it's going to be torn down to make way for new condos to house whatever characters that will inhabit the place. (Creative Time later announced that it wouldn't be condos but instead a public park.) What they collaborated on and housed inside the old plant is what makes me wonder about cultural controversy, identity formation, and the female gaze in terms of objectification.

Now, let's talk about reality first. I haven't seen the installation in person yet but there are numerous images available on the internet that make me feel as if I can describe to you what it would be like to walk into the plant. My best guess is this: as you approach the dilapidated building you are greeted by an artist statement outside to read the formal title of the work, "*A Subtlety: A Marvelous Sugar Baby, an Homage to the unpaid and overworked Artisans who have refined our Sweet tastes from the cane fields to the Kitchens of the New World.*" Walker is notorious for giving her works long ass titles. They read like poetry and often end up truncated. Then you go inside the building.

Does it still smell like sugar? Can sugar smell old?

I don't know but these are things I would think if given the chance to visit the installation. That is until I would look up and see a large, white mammy sphinx in front of me as I'm guided by the 13 little boys toward her body. There she is.

Hands on the ground.
Ass in the air.
Titties exposed with aroused nipples.
Vagina peeking out in the back.
Kerchief wrapped around a head with a wide negro nose and big negro lips.
And pure white like powdered sugar.

It's damn shocking. Actually, really fucking shocking because from what I can tell of the space is that it's dark everywhere except for openings that used to be windows and I bet she really brightens the place up too. Scattered throughout the space are what Walker calls *Banana Boys*. Life-size statues of little boys cast in sugar resin holding baskets of the same substance but looking like crystallized sugar. Their bodies were derived from tchotchkes she purchased from Amazon. They come in different colors that range from intensely dark browns to burnt umber hues that I would call redbone (a racial epitaph from my childhood). They are dotted throughout the space and around the sphinx like her children or servants to a goddess. I don't know which one but they seem to shift roles back and forth. Maybe they serve as figurative representations of Tar Baby in the 21st century.

And the sphinx herself?

She sits in the back of the old structure with a presence as grand as the original Sphinx in Egypt. *Does she have a riddle to decipher? Does she represent something to her audience? Are we her audience or her entertainment?* We, the audience, are marveled by her body and structure. *How did they do it? And is she made solely of sugar?* No. She's made of sturdy foam based on a clay replica designed by Walker and has been covered in 30 tons of powdered sugar. This technique has given her such a pristine white that it's what amps up her presence in the space.

Light can't help but to bounce itself off her body and once again we are attracted to something Walker has created. These sensual elements are what makes her work very successful in the international art world.

But back home, on the frontlines where I reside, in a place that isn't inhabited by art world patrons, saints and sinners, I become less marveled by Sugar Baby. She reminds me of struggles that involve issues of colorism, socioeconomic statuses and sexism. She reminds me of the belief that white is right. She reminds me of how much the American mainstream loves naked black bodies on display like animals at the zoo. She looks like hypersexualized black controversy. Something that repeats itself over and over again like broken records on victrolas. Oh, how I'm bored with this. **According to an article in Black Art in America I could just not look at the sculpture because art is subjective and Walker is a fucking genius.** Whatever. As artists that ass is often up for criticism from anyone at any time and in any place. Just because she's Kara E. Walker doesn't make her any different. In the late 90s, African-American artist, Betye Saar created a letter writing campaign against Walker digging deep by asking if she even hates being black herself because of the violent content and nature of her works. After this white sphinx, I can't help but to begin to wonder the same.

Since Walker is no stranger to controversial subjects, she uses it to her advantage and profits off white guilt from it. Her source material stays the same using historical image references from the Reconstruction period of the American South culturally known as the Antebellum South. She has been quoted as saying the words of the novel *Gone With The Wind* shocked her as child when her family moved to Atlanta from California. At the time of its original print, GWTW was a controversial novel because it depicted a white heroine, Scarlett O'Hara, who had to come to terms with a South that no longer existed after the Civil War. *Who would care for her? How will she marry a man to take care of her?* I don't know and I don't give too much a shit about her to care. I haven't read the book or watched the movie. All I've seen are the tears Hattie McDaniel cried when she received an Oscar for playing Mammie. Hattie didn't walk down the red carpet and she definitely wasn't allowed to walk through the front door. The Sugar Baby is a visual ode to a character like Mammie and a *supposed* metaphorical representation of the real women like her. However, over here in the real world, not the art world, Mammie still exists and she comes in different colors from different cultures. She still speaks broken or improper standard English, she's still cleaning houses and she's still taking care of someone else's children. I see her all the time waiting at bus stops, inside discount food or retail stores and standing in line at fast food establishments. People look down on her blackness as it exudes from her persona like rays of sunshine. In the mainstream media, she's a background character like a servant to the white protagonist or a sidekick villain with an ignorant attitude. She's laughable at best and nothing like Walker's white Mammie sphinx who was celebrated with food, song and dance for Creative Time's annual gala this year.

It was at this moment that I paused and the sculpture became disturbing because during the festivities I saw photo after photo of long tables covered in elaborate spreads with people laughing, talking and eating in front of Walker's great big white Mammie sphinx which glowed brightly from the back of the building. The real Mammies of the world weren't invited to this party but I'm sure they helped to serve the food and clean up. The patrons and supporters of Kara Walker were so proud to be there. They were taking photos of Sugar Baby and uploading them to social networking sites so people could see size comparisons of how big she is compared to average human height. She's 35 feet tall and 75 feet long. They were revelling in the fact that their monies would go toward proceeds to an organization whose main focus is to end slavery.

This is too much I said to myself.

This looks like a celebration of the end of all blackness as we take steps further into the age of post-blackness. And her pussy is out.

Either way, I'm disturbed. Immensely. How exactly is this an homage to the men and women workers and artisans who crafted sweet confections? How does this celebrate slaves in sugar cane fields from the colonial-era Caribbean to South Carolina, Georgia and Florida? I need to know. It seems more like a celebration of Walker's ego and what she has become. Here is where I believe our similar identities begin to separate in different directions.

My identity is based on the idea, concept and history of American blackness. The great, the good and the ugly like the Transatlantic slave trade. For me to view this sphinx, I see a complete whitewashing of the things I am so proud of in terms of blackness and the African diaspora. It makes me wonder if I even have a place within the current art world as an emerging artist and developing scholar. Sugar Baby looks down on me in her photos and all I want to do is see raw molasses drip from her head, over her nose and mouth and down her chest. As if to say that no matter how white you think you can become, you are still so black that it leaks from inside your massive curvaceous body. I also wish to see that same raw molasses drip from her exposed vagina, Let it leak to the floor to remind audiences of the sexualized violence that is committed toward women of color everyday. Being a contemporary artist informs me that if sexual violence happens to black women, violence definitely happens to Latino, Asian, Muslim, Indian women and the list goes on. All of them with varying degrees of violence committed and all of them with varying degrees of whiteness being pushed upon them. In the end, our personal female identities become distorted resulting in a representation of ourselves to appear to be like the big, white Mammy sphinx. I am not empowered by Sugar Baby. My family's history isn't empowered nor represented by Sugar Baby and these are the people she is supposed to be representing.

In my eyes, Sugar Baby is nothing more than a female figure with black body features covered in the idea of refined whiteness. Media in the 21st century has made it seem that many American and Americanized women believe they need curvy features like Beyonce and sexual appetites of porn stars. And if you're not built that way in America, you will surely know it and begin to feel inadequate because of it. As a result of the growing undercover influence of pornography, especially globally, I find that many women are choosing to objectify other women in the name of white male supremacist patriarchy. To commit the same actions of your oppressor will only continue to leave you oppressed. There can't be any freedom in this level of thinking. To make my point see the blatant exposure of Sugar Baby's aroused breasts and engorged vagina. Since the early 2000s there has been an increase of the *urban* model. I blame that increase on hip hop and when the Internet really began working its way into many black households across the US during this time. Image references helped Walker appropriate a sexualized black female body due to the type of positioning of Sugar Baby's ass in the air. It's tooted and booted, baby. Ready to be taken by any man or woman who has taken on the characteristics of an aggressive man. What could it mean for a woman to project such an ideal? It's the kind of thinking that leads women to "joke" with other women about rape. That's not very funny when so many women have such violent acts committed to them on a daily basis. From the subtle street harassment to the extreme such as rape itself. How many women in the lowly position of kitchen help have been raped by their masters? How many men have dealt with the same? Yet, Sugar Baby was created in their honor.

That isn't honorable. More like a spit in the face of the people who had to deal with the bullshit it takes to serve another human being. People who have never been paid as much as Kara Walker. People who are often taken advantage of and never get the label of genius placed upon them. No. Sugar Baby is a representation of what it takes to achieve success, what you must lose and at what cost all in the 21st century. First, you must become a sordid controversy of your own kind. Then you must align your identity to the whiteness that was created from colonialism. And last, you must reject your indigenous culture under the guidelines of whiteness because white is always right.

On the night of Creative Time's annual gala, I never saw a celebration of Kara Walker. I saw a celebration of the continuing whiteness of the art world with a white mammy in the background. Paul Mooney stated in Spike Lee's **Bamboozled** that "*everybody wants to be black but don't nobody want to be **black***." A movie about a black man that rejects his blackness for wealth and notoriety in television entertainment until his dancing and jiving Mantan representation is killed on the internet for everyone to be entertained by.

How poetic just like Sugar Baby…

The Negro As Modern-Day Spectacle: Jay-Z vs. High Art

> *The definition of performance art is a [performance](#) presented to an audience, traditionally [interdisciplinary](#). Performance may be either scripted or unscripted, random or carefully orchestrated; spontaneous or otherwise carefully planned with or without audience participation.*

I needed to see that in order to give context to what I'm about to talk about. In the end, the definition of performance became owned by one group and blurred by one man.

[Recently, Jay-Z did a pop up performance/music video shoot at Pace Gallery in New York City](#) for his single *Picasso Baby* off his 12th studio album, *Magna Carta Holy Grail*. The events that transpired was art history in the making. Never has an art space been filled with this LEVEL of hip-hop celebrity. One that is admired for his assumed humbly meager beginnings into a man making millions upon millions. Everybody loves that kind of story. The self-made millionaire is a prime example of the American dream. In America, Jay-Z is a rapper and Shawn Carter is a very intelligent businessman who enjoys art. What he represents are the new patrons on the American art scene. It's new money built from capitalizing upon hip hop culture disguised as a drug dealing tall black guy from New York.

I've been driving myself crazy as to how to approach the fact that Jay-Z was doing a music video in Pace Gallery. I was already gassed about the song since reading the lyrics in the #MCHG data mining app. In four minutes he named Picasso, Warhol, Basquiat, Condo, Rothko, Koons. Art heavyweights. GOATs. Inside the gallery, he repeated his lines over and over again for six hours to face to face with random but selected audience members. He also invited artists such as Mickalene Thomas, Fred Wilson and George Condo into his performance space. When Marina Abramovic entered the gallery space, it was as if the queen of performance art blessed him with her eccentric magic. Many people were shocked and confused that she enjoyed herself and performed with the rapper.

Every article I've read about the event since was about how he copied Marina Abramovic's 2010 MoMA performance, *The Artist is Present*. I may not know her well but what I do know is that she influenced Lady Gaga and has been the leader of experimental performance art for the past 40 years. So what's a rappin ass nigga got to do with her? Easy, really. These things:

The grand ego of the artist.
The energy created by the performance between artist and audience.
The essence of the performance itself.

They have more in common than what's seen on the surface. On the surface, some who weren't in attendance believed it to be wack because a rapper appropriated a performance artist. Hyperallergic took the moment and called it *Jay-Z Raps at Marina Abramovic, or the Day Performance Art Died*. In which the writer took time to organize the documentation of the event through various Vines, Instagrams and tweets. The highly cool and elitist underground art world has spoken. And they did not enjoy this at all. In between the videos and pics the writer organized all the negative backlash to a performance that was highly intelligent and a powerful business introduction. Lately, I've noticed that while majority of America is having a love affair with dumbing down, in between the bullshit are these pockets of superinformation geeks that devote their time to the purity of any craft. If this magazine is supposed to be sensitive to "art and its discontents" then they are doing their job well. It sounds like the same elitist art shit that been repeated since the rise of Clement Greenburg disguised as contemporary art reporting.

But I'm sleep tho. I'm also not in the mood to address the race of it all yet. That's too easy. Another nigga jiggin' in a space created by whiteness. All right. Got it. NO SHIT. See Derek Conrad Murray's *Hip-Hop vs. High Art: Notes on Race as Spectacle* for a better and in depth discussion.

On to the next.

Amongst the spectators were Jerry Saltz, a NY-based art critic that I like. He's known for dissing a lot of artists and loving who's already established. His detailed account of the performance was written more like someone who had fallen underneath the spell of a magical negro. Here in this space that Saltz knows so well, he performed himself without even knowing. He made it obvious that he didn't know much about Jay-Z in the same way I don't know much about Abramovic. From what I've learned of her performance retrospective at MoMA is that her audience participants walked away filled with emotions they couldn't express properly. Some people even walked away crying. When I learn something like that and go back to read Saltz's article I find similarities between accounts. If an emotion can be described as any strong feeling then Jay-Z's appropriation of Abramovic was successful. On a spectrum of giddy like a schoolgirl to crying my eyeballs out like a teenage girl, Saltz was giddy and even danced with Jay-Z.

Now when was the last time some shit like this went down on the art scene? Never. Not at least since the New York art scene met and danced with Jean-Michel Basquiat. Both men come from hip hop backgrounds and took a vested interest in his talent in order to succeed in a world that wasn't created for him. Like I said, Jay-Z is a rapper and Shawn Carter is an intelligent man. His artistic name dropping are from a man that seems to have recently learned more about art. And a trip through MoMA will teach anyone the same names he's rhyming about on *Picasso Baby*.

Back to the performance evaluation. Was it a blatant rip of Abramovic? Absolutely. Her participation in the event means there was a prior discussion about what his motives were for appropriating her style . Hip hop is an amalgamation of black music through American history. It will always be considered an outsider in the art world even though its aesthetic has been accepted. It's the everything else that isn't accepted because art world is this eurocentric space. I'm too much of a nigga truly be accepted or else I will appear to be performing or jiggin'.

As an example of this, I met a woman that discussed this moment in her blog, The Musings of a Renegade Futurist. Nettrice Gaskins was a PhD candidate at Georgia Tech that designed a STEAM (Science, Technology, Education, Art and Mathematics) portal for the Smithsonian in Washington, DC. In her post, *Picasso Baby: The New Society of the Spectacle*, she highlights the philosophy of Guy Debord's The Spectacle of the Society, in accordance with 20th century Situationists. Together, the spectacle of the performance becomes critiqued by know-it-alls of the art game. Debord states in his work, "The spectacle is not a collection of images, but a social relation among people, mediated by images." If I am to believe that then I can believe these two things: 1) Jay-Z was taken in as a spectacle by art world elites and 2) Jay-Z introduced a new buyer of art. Himself. Both sets, the art world and Jay-Z, have in their minds a way of seeing themselves and what they accept in their lives. The art world accepts Jay-Z as a rapper and art buyer but not as an artist even when co-signed by heavyweights. I will defend Jay-Z as an artist because we are creative and influential people. His music catalog and business ventures illustrate both.

 As Nettrice quoted Ralph Ellison at the end of her post, Jay-Z rendered the Invisible Man visible in a space that is normally devoted to whiteness. For real. Look up Pace Gallery's artist list. Fred Wilson was the only one I could find that has African roots. If the art world accepts a label such as post-black then I don't need to fuck with them. They ain't ready for the rest of blackness. They have claimed and illustrated what they accept as blackness which is the traditional slave narrative or artistic interpretations of black stereotypes. One would sooner be a security guard for a building than a celebrated, groundbreaking black artist in this industry.

We exist in a society where the negro is still a spectacle in the 21st century. Jay-Z might have been better off dancing a jig like ManTan in Spike Lee's Bamboozled. It would've been better received.

SIDE B:
9. space is the place
#nowwatching: Sun Ra - Space Is The Place
#nowplaying: Miles Davis - Bitches Brew, Parliament Funkadelic - One Nation Under a Groove

The summer I saw *Space Is The Place*, I was staying in a small house in Decatur with a friend named Friday. There were people over to house one night and a guy named Offie (like coffee and from Baltimore) had a movie he wanted all of us to see. When asked the title, he replied in a loud and excited manner, "Space is the fucking place!" I was so stoned that I never heard what he said actually and made him repeat it several times. Everyone gathered around my old television set in the living room, cut the all lights off, pressed play and sparked another blunt to be passed around. None of us knew what we were getting into and then it started... I was mesmerized by the power and charisma of Sun Ra and his musical Arkestra. I had heard his message so loud and clear in the movie that late, smoky night. I began to think he was talking to me telling me that I was a lost little black lamb. And I was because from that day I was taken away into the darkest spaces of my mind engulfed in the idea that blackness is the beginning, middle and end, a neverending cycle that equally promotes life and death.

As a result of that ganja-filled night, I have integrated the concepts, cultures and influences of Afrofuturism, Escapism, Southern Gothic and Afropunk into my works. There I am born from absolute darkness, the one in power giving birth to my creations that live to empower the colorful people of Earth.

Sun Ra was out to lunch and I don't mind going to join him.

On Afrofuturism & Escapism

> **Afrofuturism** - an emergent literary and cultural aesthetic that combines elements of science fiction, historical fiction, fantasy, Afrocentricity, and magic realism with non-Western cosmologies in order to critique not only the present-day dilemmas of people of color, but also to revise, interrogate, and re-examine the historical events of the past.
> **Escapism** - a mental diversion by means of entertainment or recreation, as an "escape" from the perceived unpleasant or banal aspects of daily life. It can also be used as a term to define the actions people take to help relieve persisting feelings of depression or general sadness.
> **Southern Gothic** - a subgenre of Gothic fiction unique to American literature that takes place exclusively in the American South. Common themes in Southern Gothic literature include deeply flawed, disturbing or eccentric characters who may or may not dabble in hoodoo, decayed or derelict settings, grotesque situations, and other sinister events relating to or coming from poverty, alienation, racism, crime, and violence.[1]

http://en.wikipedia.org/wiki/Southern_Gothic - cite_note-1

In the beginning when I was introduced to afrofuturism I thought it was dope to have niggas in space suits exploring galaxies with aliens. I didn't give it much thought until I began building the skeleton for this mythology I had started developing with Long Live the Dirty South.

Ever since then, **everything has changed**. Long Live the Dirty South is now a prototype/archetype series.

However, I am hit with a new set of problems to solve such as how big?, how small?, what am I communicating? and will my audience get it? I've gathered a new set of artists to research that utilize the concepts that I'm playing with in the works. They are Robert Pruitt, Jack Whitten, Renee Stout and Henry Darger.

Robert Pruitt's figurative works highlight people that I see in my community with an added twist. He adorns them and details them with African objects from masks to pyramids that evoke a sense of sankofa and reference American black history such as the Great Migration or the birth of hip-hop. His characters are fully aware of their present presence while acknowledging their historical pasts, ancient and new. This applies to all of his figures on paper. They wear present-day clothes while donning tribal masks they may only see in history museums or a bare bones African art section in a contemporary museum. Pruitt is looking at the past for present empowerment in the grim future of American blackness. The clothes of his characters remind me of the kind of black people that wouldn't be found in country clubs or Jack and Jill societies. They are the kind of black people that were my camp counselors, Sunday school teachers and afternoon babysitters. These people speak of blackness behind closed doors never allowing whiteness to know that they know the history of the African diaspora. These people taught me about African kings and queens before the age of consumer level internet access. Pruitt decorates their bodies with embellishments that reminds me of those almost forgotten moments.

With Jack Whitten, I find that I'm attracted to his repetition skills. Process and materials become one as he creates these active paintings. His works also remind me of the quilts of Gee's Bend because the perceived unbalanced nature of the painting is actually in balance. The repetition of squares seem to bounce in, out and off the canvas as if I'm listening to the late works of Miles Davis. Davis helped usher the concept of Afrofuturism with Sun Ra and Parliament Funkadelic. All of these musicians utilized art works for albums that illustrated the concept as well as composed music that pushed the ear into outer space and beyond. Smooth, melted together yet revealing and rhythmic. The exact same effect occurs with my eyes as I view Whitten's works because space isn't this linear thing but something happening all at once. It's chaotic yet orderly. Pitch black but filled with vibrant color.

When it comes to Henry Darger, I enjoy his works because of his strength in visual storytelling but the little kid worship turns me off. Darger looks like he was a sick fuck while he was living or a man that had an overactive imagination that I don't quite understand. What I can understand is that he had the ability to pull from pop/pulp culture and mock the false maturity of adults hence the little children everywhere in his works doing *mature* things. He was a reclusive man that didn't get recognized until after he died and someone found his 15,145-page fantasy called *The Story of the Vivian Girls, in What is Known as the Realms of the Unreal, of the Glandeco-Angelinian War Storm, Caused by the Child Slave Rebellion.* He is the king of outsider art because for his entire life he was spent on the outside looking in. I believe that to be by choice more than fear. No white man in American society is scared of anything. But he is an artist and saw a distortion in society that made him illustrate a story that few would understand. When pop/pulp culture was beginning, it was created in response to American duties of war. The public was looking for ways to escape the reality of being at war. Pop culture allowed them to forget what was happening through the beginning of celebrity worship while pulp culture celebrated topics such as fantasy, horror and science fiction. For Darger, he saw a bunch of adults acting like little children and illustrated them as such in his epic novella.

In Renee Stout's works, I find that guidance that I need to create works involving found objects. I believe that with *Of Gods & Monsters,* I am working in the similar vein as her without having to come up with different personalities to communicate what I have to say. I'm trying to create a bridge between past and present using fantasy and science fiction included in the mix because those are huge pop culture influences in my life. As mystical as her work appears to be, it reminds me of objects I've seen while antiquing with my grandmother when I was a child. There is just as much power in Stout's objects as there are in Radcliffe Bailey's *Memory as Medicine* objects. Yet, instead of being discussed on the same level, Bailey has more acclaim than Stout but the essentially create the same level of work. (Okay.) Between Bailey and Stout, I will always enjoy how they choose to utilize elements of pre-slavery religions and blackness. They make the boogeyman seem less spooky by elevating hoodoo and voodoo from forgotten religions of African-American culture to relics of power. The powerless always enjoy works of art that imbue and radiate power. See Kehinde Wiley and Mickalene Thomas. All of these artists that I've mentioned do exactly that in their own interpretations.

I have made it my goal to make *Of Gods & Monsters* reflect each and every artist that I have referenced here. It will have a bit of hoodoo, pop culture, sexuality and a lot of hip-hop. With Darger as a storytelling muse, I believe that I am now the new outsider to this 21st century art world because I don't understand many things within it. I don't understand why it's still male-centered and dominated. And I don't understand why I must make works that have to reflect feminism because I am a woman. I believe that you can discuss feminism as theory with my works but I'm never thinking of that when I work. I do, however, think about post-structuralism and cultural marxism like any other black *(post)*graduate art student.

But who really cares when people only notice you as a cute southern girl from the Carolinas. They always treat me like that. I'm bored with it and I'm 30. I'd rather write a story where I am the hero triumphing over the all black posh elite. Maybe we'll reference Spike Lee's School Daze and place them in the Realm of Wannabes. Maybe. In the end, according to Western culture, I be perceived like Eshu, a Yoruba deity that is often communicated as the devil in mainstream media because he is a trickster. Yet, he is far from it. He stands at the crossroads watching everything and everyone. He will guide some people to their rightful paths while others may be tricked to learn of their shortcomings. I am his little sister; an artistic extension. He tricked me into coming to Earth to watch the humans and learn from them and better understand them. By doing this, I can provide a different set of lens to them in order to see the bigger universal picture.

Experiencing Afropunks in ATL
I remember when I first saw him.

I think I've shared these words with him before but I know by now that we both don't remember if that to be true or not. *But, back to the statement.* When I first saw him, he was such a skinny thing that often wore a green track jacket, camouflage military hat and wore a transparent book-bag with his named typed large in a small pocket for everyone to see. FRIDAY. I thought he was a slow one and needed his name on everything in order to keep track. I later learned I was wrong. He never paid attention to me during those moments. Just heard the bellows of my laughter ringing through school halls according to him. Eventually, I met the man, the myth: Tim Friday. We became friends, shared a dorm room and a crib then burned and crashed. We just simply hung out with one another too much. There was demise and then forgiveness because I couldn't be mad at a boy like that for long. He is just too damn odd. And I liked it.

Years have passed since that friendship. I found another friend that turned into a relationship and we had a son together. Now, I just see Friday in passing every now and then across Atlanta.

In 2007, when we shared an old, little fixer-upper in Decatur. It belonged to his father and Friday allowed me to stay there as appreciation for allowing him to stay in my dorm room the previous school year. I said yes but his father was a little angry because I had no way of paying rent. I guess he figured me to be a cool person and was able to share things on his mind he felt he couldn't share with people he had known his entire life. He was questioning things I had already questioned previously such as *if I'm black, do I have to do the same things as other black people? Do I have to dress the same way as the black people in my neighborhood? Am I to only listen to rap and R&B? Do I have to go to church every Sunday dressed impeccably?* We were doing some hardcore generalizations of American black people and seriously looking for an answer to his questions. The answer I could give him was James Spooner's **Afropunk** hoping it would ease his questioning mind.

Today, he has come full circle to place that I believe a lot of black millenials are gathering. We want to be appreciated for who we are no matter our outlandish attire, colorful language usage and bizarre thought process. We've been raised by cartoons only to be desensitized by the same media. Some of us have no interest in playing basketball or football professionally just because we're black. Some of us want to ride skateboards, ride brakes-free fixed gear bikes and try our best to change the world as activists via social media. Some of us do not want to be married with kids living in a house surrounded by a white picket fence looking to join Jack and Jill groups. Most of us just simply want to be. Or at least that's what I walk away thinking after viewing Corey Davis & Sean Fahie's mockumentary, *A Day in the Life of Tim Friday*. It was written to be viewed by groups of people that would be entertained by a classic storyline such as boy meets girl, boy loses girl, boy gets girl back. It's the setting and type of character used that changes everything. A skinny black kid that plays in a punk rock band who loves riding bikes. If we were to continue to allow Hollywood to tell this story for us, he would've been a drug dealer or two-bit hustler. There are more black characters than that. Even if this story were to be told by Black Hollywood, the skinny black boy would've been some sort of Christian black boy praying to God for the perfect woman. I have nothing but vomit for both characters. They keep blackness in the 21st century monolithic and controlled.

Being raised by a old generation of African-Americans, I already know what they would think if they saw the 30 min. short. They would believe Friday to be crazy, silly and that he would need to grow up. It would be at that point I'd ask "Into what? Something he doesn't want to be so he can be miserable for the rest of his life?" I would explain to them that the point of the movie is to see a different perspective of African-American living. I'd also let them know that this is a growing group of people that are leaving behind certain traditional visuals that remind me of Cosby-style living. On the flip side, it saddens me that with all the information flying around us at all times the majority in both of these groups I'm speaking about have not realized that the Black experience is filled with a range of alternative perspectives. We have never been alone, folks. Just ignorant of the man sitting next to us on the bus.

A Day in the Life of Tim Friday actually proves that ignorance in terms of the visual identity of Atlanta to the mainstream consumer. Everyday, you hear people talking about how gay Atlanta is or how many black people live in Atlanta. Yes, Atlanta has a very large gay population and what is portrayed in mainstream about them is often incorrect as well. I often participate in the latter because there's nothing like a metropolitan city filled with black people. I often examine the spaces in between that get no shine and these spaces are occupied by some very interesting folk with stories for days. Stories about living in Atlanta and being acquainted with her variously different neighborhoods from Cabbagetown to Inman Park to the Historic West End and Bankhead. Media vehicles like WorldStarHipHop ruin Atlanta's identity by making viewers think nothing but ignorance runs rampant in her streets. I must say that if that is what you're looking for then you will surely find it in Atlanta. However, you'll miss sitting in a place like Jack's Pizza to order cheap beer, whiskey and pizza while having a conversation with working artists. You'll never see the group of black guys who meet up to ride bikes on the weekends near Paris on Ponce. You'll never meet Corey Davis, Sean Fahie or Tim Friday because you'll always be looking in the wrong spaces.

As much as black Hollywood makes up the identity of Atlanta, so do guys like these. They're peppered throughout Atlanta acting as the arms, legs, fingers and toes of the city. They are the creatives that may never get highlighted in Atlanta's especially small arts community. They carved their own spaces and have chosen to create from there. And they aren't alone because if I sat here and named names of more friends, this essay would be too damn long. A punk is not a faggot as my mother believes. That's some bullshit. An afropunk is someone who defies the monolithic, essentialist nature that has become the African-American community. We are well aware of our black history but recognize that we live in the 21st century with other cultures surrounding us. We are the *other* Black experience (as the Afropunk website states). Once this generation gets to be old, it is my hopes that to be an afropunk will be a normal identity found in American society. Right now, it's still a growing child since the 1970s as a result of the creations of A Band Called Death and Bad Brains, the earliest black punk bands which influenced and ushered in the American punk music culture/scene.

Blackness has always been othered since the rise of European imperialism later transforming into American politics. I really want purveyors, participants and owners of blackness to stop othering it and its different forms of identity. This is a learned behavior from a colonized individual. Unlearn it in the same manner that Friday unlearned a lot of things during our time together. Presently and on screen, he is the Friday that was peeking through the identity veil long ago when he first started this afropunk journey. It's funny how in hindsight, I now remember a moment when we joked about how a movie involving him would be terribly hilarious. It just so happened that Corey and Sean were there to actually make something of it.

Enjoy the film and long live the dark side that is Friday's black ass.

SIDE B:

10 - in kurt we trust: the aftermath of grunge
#nowplaying: Nirvana - You Know You're Right & Heart-Shaped Box

Whiteness and blackness have a tumultuous history. There has been so much created hatred between the two that one can miss the beautiful influential interaction that happens when the cultures collide. As quickly as I will call out the exclusion of blackness in white spaces, I can also speak about when whiteness has influenced blackness. For years, American music has been influenced by black culture. For example, rock music would not be what it is without the sounds of Son House and Chuck Berry. House brought the blues to white households when vinyls were created and distributed. Berry took the power of the guitar to another level. Since then, we've seen rock groups come and go. Elvis Presley became the first big pop star by stealing black voices. The Beatles became the first worldwide music sensation through saccharine sounds and happy pop lyrics. Both of them never caught my attention. I didn't start listening to any white rock voice until one fateful afternoon in the early 1990s. I was in someone's home watching MTV when I saw Smells Like Teen Spirit by Nirvana. The sound of the ripping guitar made noises that I had never heard. Kurt Cobain's voice wasn't dripping with molasses. He yelled and screamed at me while I moved closer and I was moved to my core by him. I felt dirty and ashamed and flipped the channel but quickly flipped back. I wanted to hear more but the video ended. The drawl of his guitar fading closed the song.

What I didn't realize until his death a few years later was how influential he would become for my style, attitude and voice. Today, if you were to walk into a karaoke joint mostly inhabited by black people and you choose to play his music, the entire room would join along. We accepted him into our lives because we clearly recognized his artistry as a man and a very frustrated American sick of American bullshit. He complained endlessly like the spoiled brats we are and we loved it. He wasn't afraid to exhibit his individuality, no matter how outlandish it seemed. We knew he was a white dude but he wasn't just any white dude. He was a brilliant artist that knew how to communicate to his audience. I was more affected by his death than the death of his musical counterparts of the time, Tupac and Biggie.

In Kurt We Trust: 20 Years Later
What is it like to live in the suburbs? It's quieter and removed from the type of folk who live in urban landscapes. I call it suburgatory like the television show currenty on ABC because what's seen on the outside is nothing like what happens on the inside. While homes stand tall and pretty, filled with furniture only seen in department stores & catalogs and shiny new cars in garages, some folk that live in these spaces are met with a type of loneliness that's like none other. There is this mind-numbing silence that walks through the neighborhood unlike living on a farm or way out in the country where you've got the musical hum of nature to keep you company. It's so quiet that it will drive you crazy. Parents work all day or night to keep the house together. Children become latch-key kids left to their own advanced technological devices to keep them company. Trouble brews in the spaces between each home. Waiting, bubbling and eventually boiling until something is unearthed or before you know it change has made a visit and nothing is the same.

Because of living in this style of environment during the early 1990s I became attracted to the sound and style of Nirvana. I was in a predominantly black middle school therefore I hid my love for this sound until a school dance during those final days before summer transitioned into high school. Then I saw many black children that had the same love that I did for Nirvana. When high school came, they were silent again while I stayed vocal in my love affair with Kurt specifically.

Grunge. Even the word sounds dirty, gritty and not very pretty.

This week marks the 20th year of Kurt Cobain's exit from planet Earth. Whether it was suicide or as some conspiracy theorists say "a set-up" he's gone and has been gone for a while. What he left behind has become this cherished, almost worshipped thing for Nirvana fans across the globe. It was his music and lyricism that has helped many of us live through these hollow suburban spaces. I know that sounds like #firstworldproblems but as long as we're living on this Earth everybody is going to go through problems.

Which brings me to Hyperallergic's The Failures of 1970s Suburban Life by blog writer, Ryan J. Simons. What I read today about 1970s artist Gordon Matta-Clark reminded me about Nirvana and Kurt Cobain. That through all the pretty that was created for suburbia, the cracks and kooks that can develop out of the human experience can never be hidden. What Simons explores during the course of this article is why suburbia has failed since the 1970s and how Matta-Clark exposed that failure by splitting abandoned houses in half. The article then begins to highlight an exhibition at Carriage Trade Gallery in SoHo, New York called *Cutting Through the Suburbs* which was organized to educate about the failures of architectural and environmental design during the post-war 1970s. The economy was sinking, the gap between rich and poor grew wider and the beginnings of hard drug abuse and PTSD made themselves known.

What does this all mean and how does it relate to Nirvana? Simple.

History loves to repeat itself over and over again. Out of some sort of an American tragedy is new art ever born in this country. Something that has never been seen before or heard before. By the time the 1970s ended, some hippies turned into intense drug addicts or become corporate slaves. We soon transitioned into the Reagan era in the 1980s and neo-conservatives were born from [trickle down economics](). The concept of suburbia was reborn and were pushed further away from cities with bigger houses and bigger toys. We were also in the golden era of pornography because VHS changed the home entertainment game. And finally [Operation Desert Storm]() under the helm of former President George Bush.

Where there is war, there's economic changes that push and pull on the American public especially for those that exist in the lands of middle and lower class.

Enter the late 1980s and early 1990s. Because of Operation Desert Storm, plenty money and opportunities had been depleted leaving many without opportunities to grow financially. Suburban homes became filled with family members that never went to college, had no dreams of pursuing any American Dreams or broken families due to broken hearts and broke wallets. The only new thing musically to rise out of America during this time was hip-hop because the hair metal/stadium rock of the 80s began to die down after pushing punk into the background.

White folks ain't know what to do. Changes were made. Feelings were hurt. Emptiness and loneliness in these suburban spaces took over and ran free. In empty garages, [grunge]() was born allowing notable bands such as Jane's Addiction, Pearl Jam and Stone Temple Pilots to become new faces to MTV.

And then there was Nirvana…

As attracted I became to this new rock sound I had heard, I became even more attracted to visuals. Stringy haired white boys in flannel plaids, old T-shirts, torn or frayed sweaters and combat boots. I wanted to be like them even though I was just 10 years old. I wanted to inhabit the spaces they frequented. I wanted to look just like them. But I was too young to know the dangers of those spaces and too bright-eyed to know the sadness behind their eyes.

Just like any other American teenager that fell in love with Nirvana, I, too was shocked when I found out that Kurt Cobain had committed suicide. At that point, I made it my mission in life to become as brilliant as he was. I wanted to explore the same dark spaces that he did in order to reek of an authenticity that represented weird America but centered in blackness. Let's all be glad that the oddities known as Outkast and Red Hot Chili Peppers saved me (and has saved me over and over again due to existing in this peculiar space). But I digress...

And history has repeated itself AGAIN. This time, war has had a bigger effect on more than just white people in suburbia. It has also severely affected the people of color that have moved to these spaces from the mid-1990s to the present. The Second Gulf War has caused a heavier strain on the American public ushering in what is known as the Great Recession during 2007. No great art or music has been born since. Hip-hop has become something quite synonymous with the glam rock of the 1970s soon to be in its hair metal age. Yet, the effects of Kurt have seeped all across American culture through the concept of the remix culture. Case in point, there's a rapper out of Texas named Kirko Bangz in which I'm sure that if Kurt were alive today, he may be disgusted with this type of appropriation or the rapper himself would have a much different sound.

Nirvana has reached beyond simple posters and T-shirts and have become a part of American history. They are the act known for changing the course of American pop music and political actions due to Krist Novoselic's JAMPAC (Joint Artists and Musicians Political Action Committee). They gave birth to Foo Fighters through the mind of Nirvana's drummer turned lead guitarist, Dave Grohl. Who knew a couple of kids from Seattle were going to do all of this? I clearly didn't at the time. And how could I if I was fucking 10 years old?

In the end, we can make this rather watered down and talk about the effects of powerful art on society. I'd rather end this by stating that Suburbia is a strange land than gives birth to intense emotions and creativity in the cracks of its broken, badly planned environmental design. Because when you're separated like that without the ability to do things as simple as farm your land or explore busy city streets/neighborhoods, you're left with a blank canvas which can either be highly creative or very destructive or both.

Beware of suburgatory.

I would never bother you
I would never promise to
I would never follow you
I would never bother you
Never speak a word again
I will crawl away for good
I will move away from here
You won't be afraid of fear
No thought was put into this
Always knew it would come to this
Things have never been so swell
I have never felt this well
Pain! [x3]
You know you're right [x3]
- Kurt Cobain, one of his last compositions written in 1993

Carla Aaron-Lopez

epilogue
#nowplaying: Road to Zion - Nas feat. Damien Marley; God's Gonna Cut You Down - Johnny Cash

You've made it to the end but a celebration doesn't begin yet. I started writing this book because at first I felt that I had things that I needed to get off my chest after having my first child. Somewhere through all of this I found a way to write a memoir-slash-cultural essay book to the sound of music, visuals of movies and words of other books. By combining all these interests a world of possibility opened up and swallowed me in. I found a way to organize my thoughts using the concept of a mixtape as a metaphor. Mixtapes are usually a collection of songs that may or may not relate musically but there is an underlying theme driving the lyrics or overall concept. How can I mix and match my words, the inspiration behind them and execute a finished project? Where else can you read about a relation between Anthony Bourdain and Beyonce? Or the justification of ratchetry in a puritan-centered culture? What about the celebration of Afropunks and niggas? It's all here. If you made it this far then you've read my perspective on it all.

Really because it all haunts me. One in a million I am with time to observe the world around me as I perform the same responsible duties as any other working adult. I get to see and hear your children talk about things you didn't know they knew. I watch as men and women change clothes to attract one another or come together to fight for what's right. I hear the sounds of the world whenever I flip through digital television and radio stations. It doesn't matter if voices are talking or singing on those stations because sometimes it all sounds the same. Deep bass, treble humming and instruments arranged to a beat. The world's influences with one another are very powerful making the voice of the individual seem quiet and alone. My book is for that individual. Let them know that I experience the same issues as you. Let them know that I have the same questions as you. We may not be heard when we ask why because life dictates that we work until we die when it doesn't have to be that way.

My best suggestion to you is try your best to keep your sanity. Will you dance with me alone in the middle of night across bodies of water and land? Do you also disagree with how women are treated where you're from? Can we finally get that beer I talked about in the prologue? I hope so. Write your thoughts down, gather them together and create a book for me to read and be inspired. Life is difficult but you don't have to feel alone because I am with you. I think about you when I write and make new art work. I love you. I gave you an intimate part of myself through these pages.

Some will disagree with me when they read these pages. I suck my teeth and say fuck you. Every single time. Some will feel my words and begin to change their minds about how they see and interact with the world. I praise your intelligence and ability to accept that which is different. The world is our playground after all but we choose to fight over who has control over that playground. No one does because our eyes stopped watching God a long time ago. Shock is no longer shocking. Being jaded is a disease. Apathy is an affliction. Babylon is real and I'm alone on the road to Zion.

At this point I end these words walking away to the sounds of Johnny Cash. His words reflecting my current moment and his music being an epitome of Americana. He's dark, reflective, spiritual and very bluesy even though he's billed as a country singer. A rebel in his own right as well. However, he was bound to be an artist and storyteller. His childhood was filled with unpleasant memories like many of us out here. I reflect on him at the moment because many of my past deeds are catching up to me feeling like God is about to cut me down. Let's go and get that beer before it happens.

You can run on for a long time

no crown, no title: a mixtape of tho(ugh)ts

Run on for a long time
Run on for a long time
Sooner or later God'll cut you down
Sooner or later God'll cut you down

Go tell that long tongue liar
Go and tell that midnight rider
Tell the rambler, the gambler, the back biter
Tell 'em that God's gonna cut 'em down
Tell 'em that God's gonna cut 'em down

End epilogue song.

www.ingramcontent.com/pod-product-compliance
Lightning Source LLC
Chambersburg PA
CBHW060418050426
42449CB00009B/2012